GEORGE W. BUSH

Texas Governor and U.S. President

Patrice Sherman

Publishing Credits

Dona Herweck Rice, *Editor-in-Chief*

Lee Aucoin, *Creative Director*

Marcus McArthur, Ph.D., *Associate Education Editor*

Neri Garcia, *Senior Designer*

Stephanie Reid, *Photo Editor*

Rachelle Cracchiolo, M.S.Ed., *Publisher*

Teacher Created Materials

5301 Oceanus Drive

Huntington Beach, CA 92649-1030

http://www.tcmpub.com

ISBN 978-1-4333-5054-2

© 2013 Teacher Created Materials, Inc.

Printed in China

Nordica.062018.CA21800491

Table of Contents

And the Winner Is...

It was the morning of December 12, 2000. Americans still did not know who their next president would be. The election had taken place over a month ago. Yet votes were still being counted!

All eyes had turned to Florida. George W. Bush appeared to have won in Florida. He had about 2,000 votes more than his **opponent**, Al Gore. But when the **margin** is that narrow, state law requires a recount. After the recount, Bush's lead was just 537 votes. Gore asked for the votes to be counted again.

Florida officials study an election ballot while recounting votes.

George W. Bush

U.S. newspapers the day after the final election results

This time, the United States Supreme Court got involved. The Court declared a recount to be unconstitutional (uhn-kon-sti-TOO-shuh-nl). Bush was finally declared the 43rd president of the United States.

Hanging Chads

A chad is a small piece of paper punched out by a voter on a paper ballot. While recounting the votes in 2000, Florida election officials saw that some chads had not been completely removed from the paper ballot. These votes were not counted. These partially removed chads came to be known as "hanging chads."

Unconstitutional

When a law is said to be unconstitutional, it means that the law violates the U. S. Constitution. The Constitution is the supreme law of the nation. If a law is unconstitutional, then it is repealed, or canceled.

A Texas Childhood
Life in Midland

George Walker Bush was born on July 6, 1946, in New Haven, Connecticut. His mother, Barbara, was excited to have her first child. She would go on to have five more children. Bush's father, George Herbert Walker Bush, would later serve as vice president and then president of the United States.

Life in Midland, Texas, was good for young Bush. In the 1950s, kids had a lot of freedom. Bush could ride his bike just about anywhere he wanted to go. He and his friends joined the local Cub Scout troop. When they wanted to raise money for **charity**, they sold candy door to door.

George H.W. and Barbara Bush with George W.

Bush in his Cub Scout uniform

Bush in his Little League uniform

George H. W. Bush served as the 41st president of the United States. Before that, he had been vice president under Ronald Reagan for eight years. During World War II, he flew 58 successful missions as a pilot in the U. S. Navy. In 2011, he received the Medal of Freedom, the highest award for a U. S. citizen.

A Legacy of Leaders

Bush's father was not the first Bush to hold a political office. Bush's grandfather, Prescott Bush, was a U. S. senator from Connecticut. He was very involved in social matters.

Bush's favorite hobby was playing baseball. He played Little League baseball when he was a boy. He would go on to play in college. Later, in 1989, he would own the Texas Rangers baseball team!

Prescott and George H. W. Bush

Another Side of Life

Bush's childhood was not always happy. In 1953, his three-year-old sister, Robin, became ill with cancer. His parents took her to New York for the best treatment. Bush was seven years old at the time. He often stayed with friends and he did not see his parents much during this time.

Robin died a few months later. It was a sad and lonely time for the family. Bush noticed his mother's sadness. He would try to cheer her up. He would tell her his favorite jokes.

the Bush family, 1956

Bush and his mother shared the same sense of humor and the same quick temper. They both said whatever was on their minds. They were very close. His mother was the Den Mother for his Cub Scouts troop. She kept score at Bush's Little League baseball games. And she always encouraged her son to do his best.

Barbara Bush

Bush, age 9, with his parents, 1955

First Lady of Literacy

Barbara Bush was First Lady of the United States from 1989 to 1993. She used her position to promote literacy, or the ability to read. In 1990, she published *Millie's Book*, a story about the Bush family's dog Millie and her puppies. Several schools in Texas have been named in honor of the former First Lady.

Another Bush

Bush was not the only one to follow his father into politics. His younger brother, Joseph, or Jeb for short, served as governor of Florida from 1999 to 2007.

Bush standing behind his family in Houston, Texas

Phillips Andover Academy

A Bigger World

In 1959, the Bush family moved to Houston, the biggest city in Texas. Bush missed the smaller city of Midland. Houston was huge. But he soon got used to his new school. He made friends and started playing golf, a game he would play for the rest of his life.

Two years later, Bush faced an even bigger change. He attended high school at Phillips Andover Academy in Massachusetts. Both his father and grandfather had gone there. Andover was very formal. Students were expected to wear jackets and ties in the dining hall. Bush did not like getting dressed up. He would often show up for dinner wearing sneakers and a wrinkled shirt.

Bush had to work hard for passing grades. It was a challenge, but he was not a quitter. He played baseball and organized the school's stickball league. After graduating in 1964, he headed to Yale University. This is where his father had gone to college.

Bush as head cheerleader at Andover, 1964

JFK

John F. Kennedy became the 35th president in 1961. This was the same year Bush entered Andover. Kennedy was **assassinated** (uh-SAS-uh-NEYT-id) on November 22, 1963. Lyndon (LIN-duhn) B. Johnson, the vice president and a native of Texas, became the country's next president.

Change Comes to Texas

While Bush was away at school in the 1960s, Texas experienced social changes. Like the rest of the country, Texas witnessed the struggle for civil rights during these years. African Americans protested unfair laws to receive equal rights.

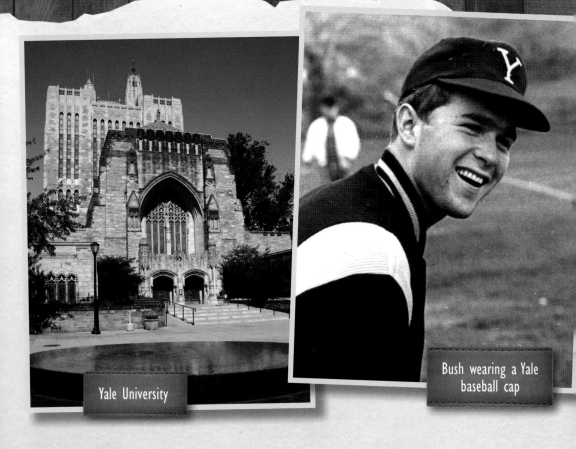

Yale University

Bush wearing a Yale baseball cap

Finding His Own Way
College Years

Like Phillips Andover, Yale was a family tradition. Bush's father, grandfather, and most of his uncles had gone there. Bush did not want to go there. But when his best friend got in, they decided to room together.

Bush was not always the best student. But he enjoyed his courses at Yale. He majored in history. One of his favorite classes was history of the Soviet Union. He also joined many groups. One group was called Skull and Bones. This was one of Yale's famous secret societies.

Bush also enjoyed his speech class at Yale. He would put these skills to work later in his career.

After graduating in 1968, Bush tried out several careers. He had followed his family tradition in his schooling. Now, Bush wanted to make his own way in life. He worked for a farming business in Texas. Then, he served in the **National Guard**.

Bush climbs the steps of a fighter plane in 1968 while in the National Guard.

The Soviet Union

Under **Communism** (KOM-yuh-niz-uhm), all property belonged to the state. Individuals had little freedom to speak or worship as they chose. The Soviet Union was a communist state that formed in Russia in 1922. In 1991, the Soviet Union ended. It was no longer a Communist country. It became known once again as Russia.

Enter the Tomb

Skull and Bones holds its secret meetings in a mysterious building called the Tomb. Members are "Bonesmen" and can join only when invited or "tapped." Yale became coed, educating both men and women, in 1969. But women students were not tapped, or asked to join the group, until 1992.

Ronald Reagan

The Reagan Years

Bush's father served as vice president under Ronald Reagan. Reagan served as president from 1981 to 1989. He believed strongly in freedom and democracy. In 1987, he called upon the Soviet Union to end communism and tear down the Berlin Wall.

Always a Teacher

Laura Welch was a librarian and an elementary school teacher before she married Bush. After Bush became president, she traveled around the world to promote the importance of education for girls and women.

Settling Down

Bush earned a **master's degree** from Harvard Business School in 1975. He returned to Midland, Texas, and started working for an oil company. In 1977, a friend introduced him to Laura Welch. She was a librarian who worked in Austin.

George and Laura on their wedding day

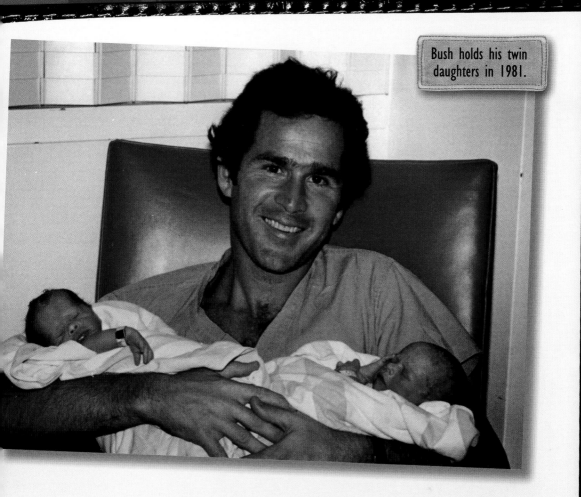

Though George and Laura had both grown up in Midland, they had never met. He was outgoing and liked to go to parties. She was quiet and liked to read. A few months later, they were married. In 1981, Laura gave birth to twin girls, Jenna and Barbara.

In 1986, at the age of 40, Bush went through a **spiritual awakening**. He had a deep talk with a famous Christian minister named Billy Graham. This talk inspired Bush to start taking both his faith and life more seriously. He felt that his new lifestyle made him a better husband and father. This was a major turning point in his life.

The Political Bug
Like Father, Like Son

Bush worked on his father's presidential **campaigns** in 1988 and 1992. Bush liked politics. But he still did not consider himself to be a **politician** (pol-i-TISH-uhn). His father was the family politician. Bush's father was vice president for eight years. Then he was president for four years. But his father's loss to Bill Clinton in 1992 changed Bush's mind. His father had settled down to live a private life. Bush felt he could now enter politics on his own terms. Bush had finally caught the political bug.

George H.W. Bush with his family during the 1992 presidential election

In 1994, Bush ran for governor of Texas. He ran against Anne Richards, a Democrat. He won by a wide margin. One of his first acts as governor was to sign a bill that allowed Texans to carry guns.

Bush's policies were moderate, or not extreme. They were a balance between Republican and Democratic policies. Bush was reelected in 1998. He served as Texas governor two terms in a row. He was the first Texan to do this.

The Right to Bear Arms

The Second **Amendment** to the U. S. Constitution in the Bill of Rights gives citizens "the right to bear and keep arms." People interpret this in different ways. Bush believed his bill protected Texans' constitutional right to bear arms.

Governor Bush

When Bush ran for governor of Texas, he promised to improve education, welfare, and Texas laws. Welfare is giving money or other things to people in need. While in office, Bush worked with Democrats to pass laws that made changes in these areas. He also cut taxes, which is the money Texans have to give the government.

The Bush family celebrates after the 1998 Texas governor election.

Running for President

In 1999, Bush decided to run for president. Bush chose Dick Cheney as his running mate. This means that Cheney would be vice president if Bush won. Cheney had been the **secretary of defense** under Bush's father. Bush and Cheney were Republicans. They ran against Democrats Al Gore and Joe Lieberman.

Bush and Cheney campaign with their wives.

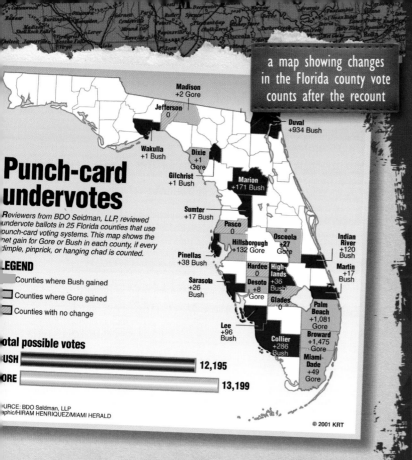

a map showing changes in the Florida county vote counts after the recount

Punch-card undervotes

Reviewers from BDO Seidman, LLP, reviewed undervote ballots in 25 Florida counties that use punch-card voting systems. This map shows the net gain for Gore or Bush in each county, if every dimple, pinprick, or hanging chad is counted.

LEGEND

Counties where Bush gained

Counties where Gore gained

Counties with no change

Total possible votes

BUSH	12,195
GORE	13,199

Madison +2 Gore
Jefferson 0
Duval +934 Bush
Wakulla +1 Bush
Dixie +1 Gore
Gilchrist +1 Bush
Marion +171 Bush
Sumter +17 Bush
Pasco 0
Hillsborough +132 Gore
Osceola +27 Gore
Indian River +120 Bush
Pinellas +38 Bush
Hardee 0
Highlands +36 Bush
Martin +17 Bush
Sarasota +26 Bush
Desoto +8 Gore
Glades 0
Palm Beach +1,081 Gore
Lee +96 Bush
Collier +286 Bush
Broward +1,475 Gore
Miami-Dade +49 Gore

SOURCE: BDO Seidman, LLP
Graphic/HIRAM HENRIQUEZ/MIAMI HERALD

© 2001 KRT

The Electoral College

The president is not elected directly by the voters. Each state has a certain number of electoral representatives based on its population. The candidate who wins the most **popular votes** in the state gets all the electoral votes. The representatives are known as the Electoral College.

It's My Party!

A political party is a group of citizens who work together to elect candidates who support its ideas. To start a political party, one has to fill out a registration form and gather a certain number of signatures on a **petition**.

The election was very close. For five weeks, the vote count in Florida was unclear. Gore had won the most votes in the nation. But he did not have enough **electoral votes** to win. Finally, Bush was declared the winner in Florida. This win gave him one more than the 270 electoral votes needed for victory.

Bush was watching TV at home when he learned he had won. In his victory speech, Bush asked Republicans and Democrats to work together. He wanted to be a uniter, not a divider.

An elephant is the symbol of the Republican Party.

September 11, 2001
A Day of Tragedy

On the morning of September 11, 2001, an airplane flew into the North Tower of New York's World Trade Center. At first, people thought it was a terrible accident. Then, 17 minutes later, another plane flew into the South Tower. Soon, a third jet crashed into the Pentagon. This is the home of the United States Department of Defense. It is located just outside of Washington, DC.

All planes in the air over the United States were ordered to land right away. One did not do so. Minutes later, that plane crashed into a field in Pennsylvania. Everyone aboard died. What was happening?

the Twin Towers shortly after the attack on September 11, 2001

Bush learns of the attack while reading to school children in Florida.

A few days later, Americans learned that al-Qaeda (al-KEY-duh) had carried out the attacks. Al-Qaeda was a **radical** Muslim group based in the Middle East. **Terrorists** had taken over the planes by force. In the fourth plane, passengers bravely fought back. They forced the plane to crash. Most people think this plane was headed for Washington, DC.

A total of 2,996 people died in the attacks on September 11. Americans were scared and confused. They turned to their president for answers.

The Twin Towers

Until September 11, the twin towers of the World Trade Center were the tallest buildings in New York City. Completed in 1973, they stood 1,365 feet (416 m) high. They each had 110 floors!

Islam

Islam (is-LAHM) is one of the world's major religions. Followers of Islam are called Muslims. Like Christianity and Judaism, Islam is a **monotheistic** (mon-uh-thee-IS-tik) religion. This means its followers worship only one god.

Bush signs the Patriot Act.

The Home Front

On the evening of September 11, President Bush addressed the nation. "Our way of life, our very freedom came under attack," he said. Bush said it was the work of terrorists. National security was his top priority. He formed the Department of Homeland Security. This group protects the United States from terrorist acts. It works closely with the Federal Bureau (BYOOR-ooh) of Investigation (FBI) and the Central Intelligence Agency (CIA).

The Patriot Act was made to fight terror. This act gave officials more power to fight terror at home. But some people did not like this law. They said it took away people's freedoms. Others said it was needed in a time of war. Both Democrats and Republicans in Congress supported the Patriot Act.

On September 14, Bush visited the site of the former World Trade Center, or Ground Zero. As he was leaving, a woman pressed a badge into his hand. It had belonged to her son, George Howard. He was a police officer who had died in the attack. Bush carried the badge with him for the rest of his presidency.

Bush holds George Howard's badge while addressing Congress.

American Heroes

Between the time that the first airplane struck and the last tower fell, hundreds of firefighters showed their bravery. Even though the towers were burning, firefighters rushed up the stairs to save people. In the end, 343 firefighters gave their lives helping the victims of the September 11 attack.

FBI and CIA

The FBI is part of the United States Department of Justice. It investigates federal crimes committed inside the United States. The CIA gathers information about activities of groups outside the United States. The CIA is often involved in spying.

War on Terror

Soon after September 11, U.S. officials learned that Osama bin Laden (oh-SAH-muh bin LAHD-n) was the leader of al-Qaeda. They also learned that the group was based in Afghanistan (af-GAN-uh-stan). A **militant** Islamic group called the *Taliban* (TAL-uh-ban) ruled Afghanistan. On September 20, 2001, Bush demanded that the Taliban hand Bin Laden over to the United States or face war. The Taliban refused. On October 7, U.S. forces and a coalition (koh-uh-LISH-uhn), or joint force, from other countries invaded Afghanistan.

Relations between the United States and Iraq (ih-RAHK) had been tense for many years. Saddam Hussein (sah-DAHM hoo-SEYN), Iraq's dictator, allowed little freedom. Bush felt it would be best to overthrow Hussein.

Bush explains the NCLB act in 2006.

AIDS

Auto immune Deficiency Syndrome, or AIDS, is a disease that has taken many human lives. There is no cure for AIDS. But doctors have developed drugs that help people live long lives even with the disease.

Bush also reformed, or changed, public education. The No Child Left Behind (NCLB) act called for more testing. The act tried to help students meet set standards. Not all people agreed that these tests would help students. Yet many agreed that American schools needed change.

Another First Lady of Literacy

Like Bush's mother, his wife Laura focused on education and literacy during her time as First Lady. With the help of the Library of Congress, Laura Bush started the National Book Festival. She has also written a children's book with her daughter, Jenna, called *Read All About It!*

Laura and Jenna Bush showing people their book

DECISION POINTS

GEORGE W.
BUSH

Bush poses while
signing his book.

Private Citizen

U. S. presidents can only serve two terms. In January 2009, Bush's second term drew to a close. He and Laura made plans to return to Texas. They settled in Dallas.

Bush tried to do what was best for the United States. He did not worry about how much criticism his decisions received. His presidency had been marked by controversy on many issues. Bush wrote his **memoirs** (MEM-wahrz). *Decision Points* became a best seller. It gave Bush a chance to explain why he made certain decisions.

George W. Bush led the United States through many challenges. The country faced its worst attack on American soil. It waged two wars. People did not always agree with his policies. But President Bush always did what he thought was best for the country.

Former President Bush speaks at a ceremony for the George W. Bush Presidential Center.

Haiti Relief

On January 12, 2010, a large earthquake hit Haiti (HEY-tee). More than 300,000 people died. Another 300,000 were seriously injured. And around one million people lost their homes. President Barack Obama asked former presidents George W. Bush and Bill Clinton to lead the U. S. relief effort. They started a fund to help Haiti.

Presidential Libraries

Each presidential library serves as the official **repository** (ri-POZ-i-tawr-ee) of documents from a president's work and life. As of 2012, there were 13 such libraries in the United States. The George W. Bush Presidential Center at Southern Methodist University in Dallas honors the life and career of George W. Bush.

Glossary

amendment—a change added to the U. S. Constitution

assassinated—killed, especially a political leader

campaigns—series of events to get voters to vote for a candidate for public office

charity—a fund for giving aid to the needy

Communism—a political system that gives all property to a central government

electoral votes—votes cast by members of the Electoral College

malaria—a disease spread by a breed of mosquito and causing extreme weakness

margin—the difference in amount

master's degree—a degree stating that classes beyond a normal college degree have been completed

memoirs—written records of one's memories

militant—engages in fighting

monotheistic—believing in one god

National Guard—state military forces that are called in when assistance is needed

opponent—a person who is on the other side in a contest or election

petition—a written request, often signed by many people, asking authorities to take a particular course of action

politician—a person who runs for or holds public office

popular votes—votes of the general public

radical—extreme

repository—a place for keeping important documents

secretary of defense—a person who organizes military action for the president

spiritual awakening—a personal realization of the necessity of spirituality

terrorists—people who cause terror in others

tuberculosis—a disease caused by bacteria, making it difficult to breathe

Index

DECISION POINTS

GEORGE W.
BUSH

Your Turn!

George W. Bush was born into an important Texas family. He became a businessman and a politician. In 2000, he was elected president of the United States. He led the nation during difficult times and was forced to make many tough decisions.

Working Titles

The title of George W. Bush's memoir is *Decision Points*. Brainstorm a list of at least five other possible titles for Bush's autobiography.